# Christmas

I0880151

## The Birth of Jesus

We learn about Jesus
when it is Christmas.

We go to church
when it is Christmas.

Holy Trinity Church of England Moe
VICAR : THE REVEREND C.J CHAMBERS 1893
Evensong 7.00 pm
NOTICES

We have a nativity
when it is Christmas.

We sing carols

when it is Christmas.

Counts

We have a tree
when it is Christmas.

We have presents

when it is Christmas.

We have pudding

when it is Christmas.

Christmas is special for us.